CATERPILLAR COUNTER

Clem the caterpillar is inching his way around this math path. Starting at any point, help him move clockwise around the garden by putting in the numbers that will solve each separate equation. Some numbers have already been put in to help guide you and Clem.

Illustrated by Liisa Chauncy Guida

Answer on page 47.

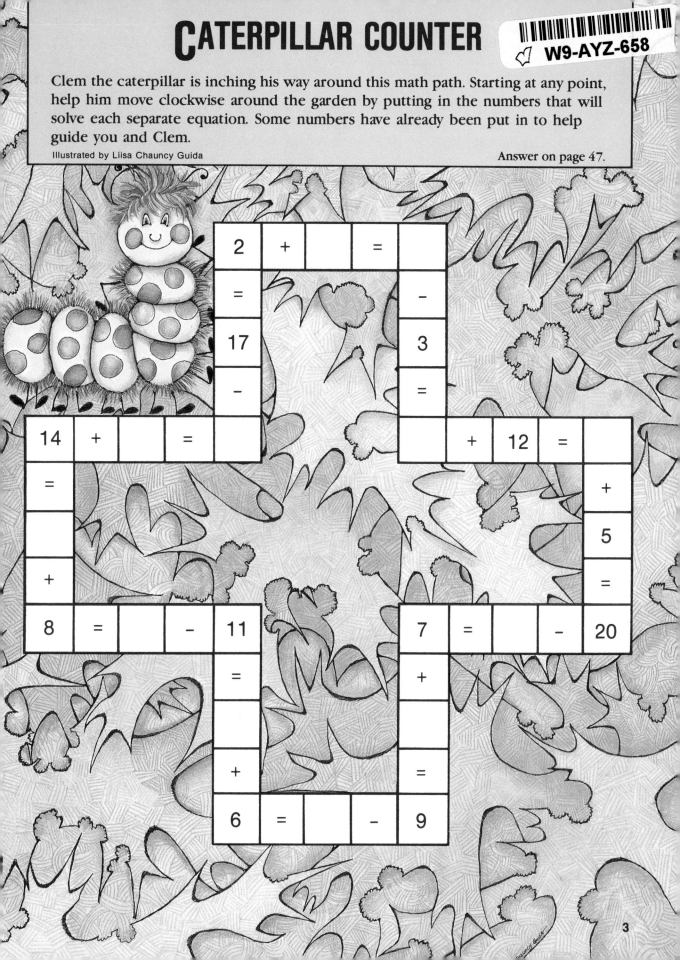

| 2 | + | | = | |

=			-	
17			3	
-			=	

| 14 | + | | = | | | + | 12 | = | |

=									+
									5
+									=

| 8 | = | | - | 11 | | 7 | = | | - | 20 |

		=			+
		+			=
		6	=		-	9

3

PAINT PUZZLE

Pete Casso, the famous artist, is painting his latest masterpiece. Brush up on your artwork as you try to find where all these words belong on Pete's easel. Use the size of the words as clues to figure out where they get painted in. Be sure to cross off each word as you use it. Pete has already started the first word.

6 LETTERS

CANVAS
CRAYON
CREATE
ENAMEL
MODERN
MUSEUM
PAINTS
SHADOW
SKETCH

7 LETTERS

ACRYLIC
CLASSIC
GALLERY
PALETTE
PASTELS
PICTURE
SCENERY
TEXTURE

5 LETTERS

BRUSH
CHALK
COLOR
EASEL
FRAME
IMAGE
LIGHT
LINES
MODEL
PAPER
SHAPE
SMOCK
STAND
TUBES

3 LETTERS

ART
INK
MIX
OIL
PEN

4 LETTERS

DRAW
FLOW
FORM
TONE
VIEW

Illustrated by John Nez

SCENERY

Answer on page 47.

ROW, ROW, ROW

Each scene of a winter holiday has something in common with the two others in the same row. For example, in the top row across, it is snowing in each scene. Look at the other rows across, down, and diagonally. What does each row have in common?

Answer on page 47.

INSTANT PICTURE

Here's a welcome sight. To shed a little light on what's hidden on this page, fill in each section that contains two dots.

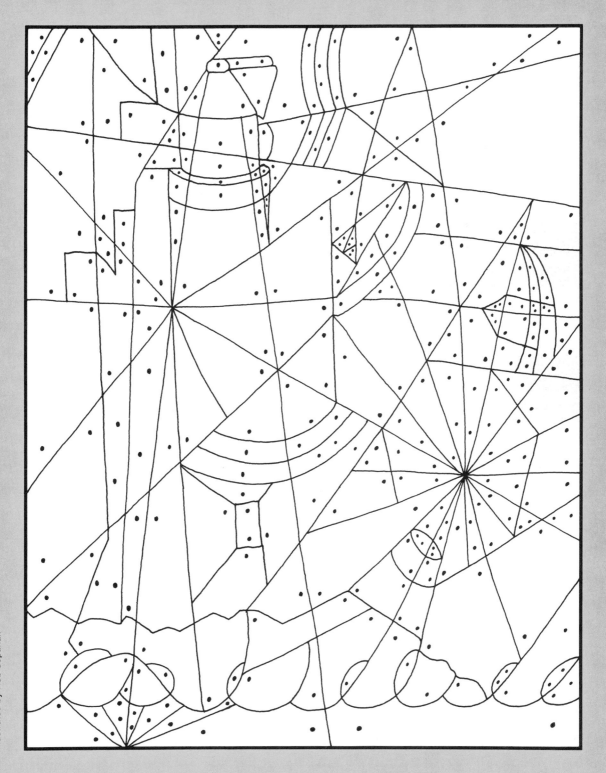

Illustrated by Rob Sepanak

HIDDEN PICTURES

There are at least 32 objects hidden in this picture.
How many can you find?

WALKIE-TALKIES

These people all walk while they talk, but they don't watch where they're walking when talking. Now they're so tangled, they don't know which receiver gets hung up where. Can you follow the wires to match each receiver with its base?

Answer on page 47.

Illustrated by Gregg Valley

BLUEPRINT BLUNDERS

Builder Bill just got the layout for his latest project. But this blueprint has a lot of mistakes in it. See if you can unscramble all the wrong words to find out what Bill is supposed to be building.

Get one GOLN piece of ODOW.

UCT out VEFI sections of equal ZESI, each ENO foot by ENO foot.

Drill a ELOH in the DIMDEL of ENO of these sections. This will be SEUD as the RONFT.

SUE another section as the SEBA. Carefully LAIN the other RUFO sections to the sides to form a OXB.

Now UCT a section WELVET inches by NETEGHIE inches. LAIN this to the top of the OXB with the extra XIS inches hanging over the RONFT.

Add a WELDO as a CHERP, and you'll have a brand new DRIBUHOSE.

Illustrated by Terry Rogers

Answer on page 47.

1

FARM FUN

It's harvest time on the farm. Time to bring in the big crop of farming words planted in the letters on the next page. See if you can pick them all out by looking up, down, across, backward, or diagonally. When you've found each word and crossed it off the list, the leftover letters will spell out some familiar farming information.

AXE
BALES
BARN
BIN
BUGS
CAN
CAT
CHICKENS
CORN
COWS
CROPS
DOG
DUCKS

EGG
FARMER
FEED
FENCE
FIELDS
FLOWERS
GEESE
GOAT
GRAIN
HARVEST
HAY
HOE
HOG
HORSES
LOFT
MICE
MILK
MUD

OATS
OWL
PAIL
PIES
PIGS
PITCHFORK
PLANTING
PLOW
POND
PUMP
RAIN
RAKE
ROOSTER
SCARECROW
SEED
SHEEP
SHOVEL
SILO

SOW
SPADE
STALL
STEER
STY
SUN
TRACTOR
TREES
TROUGH
WELL
WHEAT
WOODPILE
WORK

Illustrated by Melvin Conrad

F O L P L A N T I N G W H E A T
I E A I S T A L L P E E H S X R
E I N T R O U G H O E D D M A A
L C D C H I C K E N S E N O N C
D R A H E A O L D D E P U M P T
S L O F T T R E E S O I S I L O
K G H O A D N V C A G G E L O R
C H O R S E S A E W O S N K W E
U R A K E T R F F S A S P A D E
D S T Y A E E A G R T H L S C T
U K S S C B A R N F L O W E R S
M R W R B M A M I C E V O L O G
W O O D P I L E A L L E W A P U
C W E I N E N R R I O L D B S B

Leftover letters: _____

THE WILD WEST

During their last robbery, the Dalton Gang accidentally dropped a set of pictures that showed the way to their hideout. Now, Sheriff Sam is hot on their trail. The problem is that the pictures are all out of order. Can you figure out which order they go in so that the sheriff can corral these outlaws? Hint: Sheriff Sam knows that A is the first photo of this trail.

Illustrated by Jon Davis

E

F

G

H

I

J

K

L

WHAT AM I?

Can you guess the answer
before you reach the last clue?

1. I am a member of the family Leporidae, and the order Lagomorpha.

2. I prefer to live with others of my kind in colonies.

3. I have a life span of about ten years.

4. I eat mainly herbs, tree bark, and vegetables.

5. There are both wild and domestic varieties of me.

6. The ten well-established domesticated varieties of me are Angora, Belgian, Dutch, Himalayan, Lop, Siberian, Patagonian, Silver-tip, Polish, and Flemish.

7. I warn others of danger by thumping on the ground with my back feet.

8. Many people confuse me with my cousin, the hare, who is usually bigger and has longer ears.

What Am I?

Illustrated by Barbara Gray

Answer on page 48.

DOT'S DEPARTMENT STORE

Can you join the dots to see what things the Buntings bought when they went shopping?

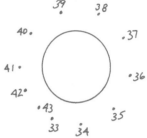

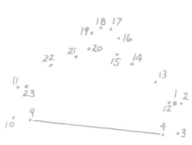

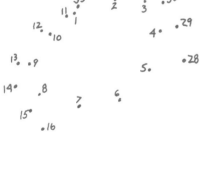

FOOD FOR THOUGHT

Chef Chuck wanted to leave a message for Ginger, the baker, but he couldn't find any paper. He used some of the food in the kitchen to develop a special code. Ginger gobbled it up as she tried to guess Chuck's message. Using the key below, see if you can figure out what Chuck had to say. Then decipher Ginger's answer.

A =

B =

C =

D =

E =

F =

G =

H =

I =

J =

K =

L =

M =

N =

O =

P =

Q =

R =

S =

T =

U =

V =

W =

X =

Y =

Z =

Illustrated by R. Michael Palan

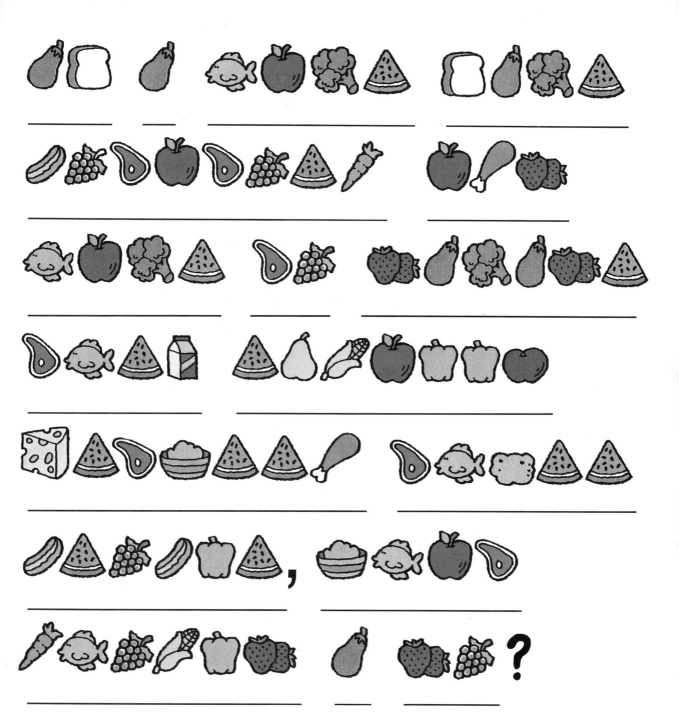

Answer on page 48.

CATEGORY CAPER

Lulu loves lists. She's sorting some stuff but doesn't know what category she should list the things under. You can help her by choosing the one word in each set that would make a good category for the other items in the same set.

1
squares
circles
triangles
shapes

2
dogs
poodles
beagles
collies

3
minnow
fish
shark
tuna

4
ferns
plants
moss
grass

5
jacket
shirt
clothing
shorts

6
dolls
blocks
trucks
toys

Illustrated by Barbara Gray

Answer on page 48.

STILT STUNT

The Bumbling Brothers circus is back in town, and one of its acts is headed for the big top. Use your imagination to draw in whoever's walking on the silly stilts.

Illustrated by Rob Sepanak

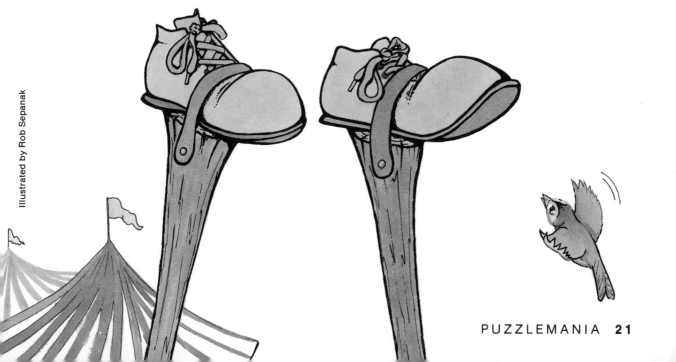

SEA CHOOSE

The annual charity sailing race brings out all types of special boats. But this year there are two pairs of boats that match. Catch a breeze and sail through this puzzle by choosing both sets of similar ships.

Answer on page 48.

Illustrated by Paul Richer

TABLE TROUBLE

Last Sunday, Ginny Lou had several friends over for a buffet dinner. On one table she set up eight different foods. From the clues, can you figure out what item goes on which plate? The foods are: turkey, roast beef, apple pie, salad, soup, steamed vegetables, rice, and gravy.

1. The turkey and roast beef are at one end of the table; the apple pie is at the opposite end.

2. The soup is directly across from and one number less than the salad, and directly to the left of the gravy.

3. The steamed vegetables are in an even-numbered position, but not in #6 or #4.

4. The rice is next to the turkey.

Answer on page 48.

Illustrated by Jon Davis

SQUARE DANCE MEMORIES

Take a long look at this picture. Try to remember everything you see in it. Then turn the page, and try to answer some questions about it without looking back.

DON'T READ THIS UNTIL YOU HAVE LOOKED AT "Square Dance Memories—Part 1" ON PAGE 25.

SQUARE DANCE MEMORIES Part 2

Can you answer these questions about the square dancing scene you saw? Don't peek!

1. Were there decorations on the wall?
2. Who was standing in the corner?
3. How many people were wearing hats?
4. What color bandana was around the man's neck?
5. How many hay bales were in this scene?
6. How many people were on stage?
7. Was anyone calling the moves at the microphone?
8. What color were the fiddler's sneakers?
9. What animal was in the scene?

Answer on page 48.

WHAT IS IT?

Do you know what this girl is talking about?

I know something that has a bank, but never any money.
It has a mouth, but never eats,
And a bed, but never sleeps.

What is it?

Answer on page 48.

Illustrated by John Nez

WHAT'S IN A WORD?

On Halloween, children go out for goodies. But did you ever notice all the goodies hiding in the letters of HALLOWEEN, like HALL? There are at least 35 words of three letters or more masked here. Don't be tricked. Get a treat by seeing how many words you can find in HALLOWEEN.

Illustrated by Anni Matsick

Answer on page 48.

THE CASE OF THE WANDERING WRENS

See if you can solve this mystery. Read the story and fill in the missing words. Then match the numbered letters with the corresponding spaces at the end of the story. If you've filled in the spaces correctly, you'll discover the answer to this problem.

It was nesting time. Wilma Wren selected a spot under the eaves of a small

white house. Using twigs from under the big maple __ __ __ __ , Wilma
                            26 12

constructed a cozy __ __ __ __ . There she laid six small __ __ __ __ .
            8   6   4

Her warm body kept them safe from the hot rays of the __ __ __ , the
                                  1

strong gales of the __ __ __ __ , and the chilly drops of __ __ __ __ .
          20   16

One day she heard a pecking sound; the delicate __ __ __ __ __
               7 22

cracked open, and six __ __ __ __ birds appeared. All six had their
       19 10

__ __ __ __ __ __ wide open, so Wilma spread her __ __ __ __ __ and
25   2

flew off to find food. It took some time, but eventually, right next to a four-

leaf __ __ __ __ __ , she spied a long, juicy __ __ __ __ . Wilma
    24 11   18

pulled it out of the ground, and flew happily toward the nest and her hungry

children.

Illustrated by Terry Rogers

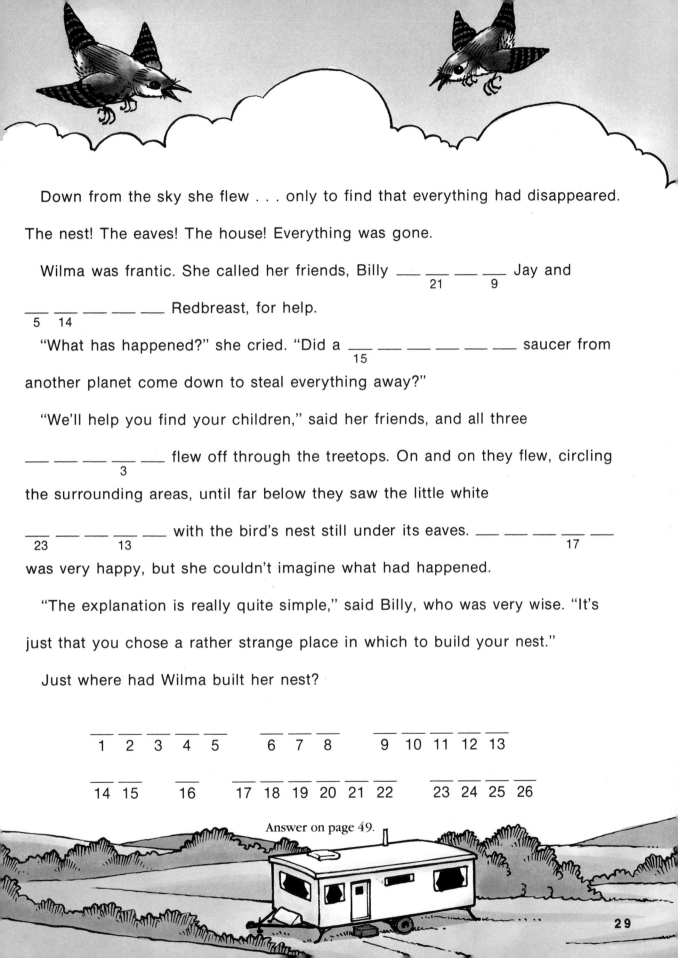

Down from the sky she flew . . . only to find that everything had disappeared.

The nest! The eaves! The house! Everything was gone.

Wilma was frantic. She called her friends, Billy __ __ __ __ Jay and
                                                  21   9

__ __ __ __ __ Redbreast, for help.
5 14

"What has happened?" she cried. "Did a __ __ __ __ __ __ saucer from
                                         15

another planet come down to steal everything away?"

"We'll help you find your children," said her friends, and all three

__ __ __ __ __ flew off through the treetops. On and on they flew, circling
        3

the surrounding areas, until far below they saw the little white

__ __ __ __ __ with the bird's nest still under its eaves. __ __ __ __ __
23   13   17

was very happy, but she couldn't imagine what had happened.

"The explanation is really quite simple," said Billy, who was very wise. "It's

just that you chose a rather strange place in which to build your nest."

Just where had Wilma built her nest?

__ __ __ __ __   __ __ __   __ __ __ __ __
1 2 3 4 5   6 7 8   9 10 11 12 13

__ __   __   __ __ __ __ __ __   __ __ __ __
14 15   16   17 18 19 20 21 22   23 24 25 26

Answer on page 49.

MUSHROOM MUDDLE

This scene is filled with at least 35 mushrooms. How many can you find?

Illustrated by Barbara Gray

STOP, LOOK, AND LIST

Under every category, list one thing that begins with each letter. For example, one thing with a hole that begins with "B" is a bowling ball. See if you can name another.

Things with Holes

B _____

C _____

L _____

P _____

S _____

Green Vegetables

B _____

C _____

L _____

P _____

S _____

Pieces of Jewelry

B _____

C _____

L _____

P _____

S _____

Illustrated by Lisa Dayer

Answer on page 49.

PICTURE MIXER

Copy these mixed-up squares in the spaces on the next page to put this picture back together. The letters and numbers tell you where each square belongs. The first one, A-3, has been done for you.

Illustrated by Rob Sepanak

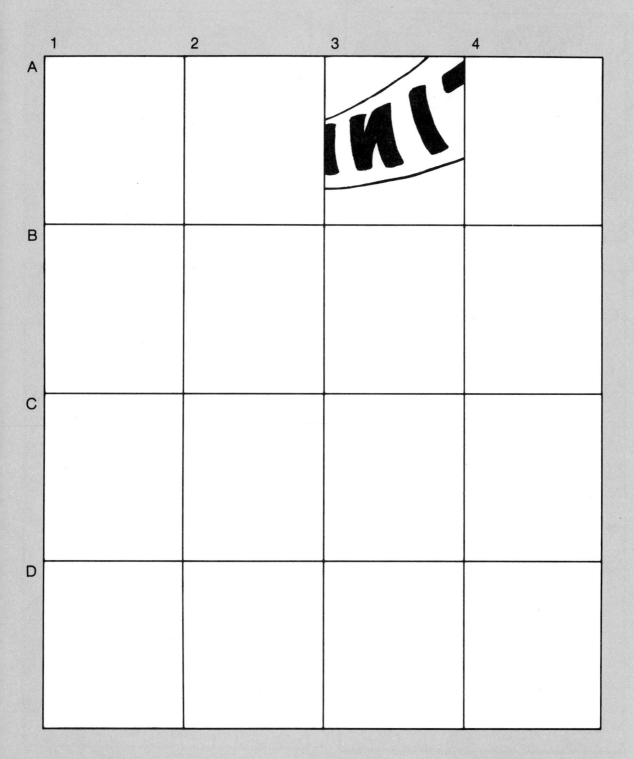

PUPPETS ON PARADE

Can you number these pictures to tell what
happened first, second, and so on?

Answer on page 49.

Illustrated by Terry Rogers

ONE MORE TIME

Count down this clue list to find all the words that have the letters ONE in them. You'll be a real Number One puzzle solver if you get every one.

1. ice cream holder   __ one

2. finished   __ one

3. skeleton part   __ one

4. vanished   __ one

5. sticky syrup   __ one __

6. coins and bills   __ one __

7. by yourself   __ __ one

8. rocks   __ __ one __

9. not later   __ __ one __

10. king's chair   __ __ __ one

11. truthful   __ one __ __

12. stranded on an island   __ __ __ __ one __

13. device for talking   __ __ __ __ __ __ one

14. musical instrument   __ __ __ __ __ __ one

Answer on page 49.

Illustrated by Paul Richer

FANCY ANTS

A colony of ants are scattered throughout this puzzle. These insects appear where the letters ANT should go. As you are solving this puzzle, draw in each ant when you find it. Two words have been done as an example. Hint: Ant does not appear in every word.

Across:

1. Tricks or pranks
4. Yarn from sheep
7. Ending for "baby" or "child"
8. Trousers
9. A cloak, or a shelf above a fireplace
11. To recline
14. Fifth note of the scale
15. Not wealthy
16. Intravenous (abbreviation)
18. United Nations (abbreviation)
19. To mend a hole in a sock
21. You and me
23. Five minus four
24. Grown-up tadpole
26. Also, or along with
28. Internal Revenue Service (initials)
30. A small whirlpool
31. Puts into soil, things that grow

Down:

1. Against
2. Word ending for "patriot" or "national"
3. Sings over and over
4. To wish for
5. Capital of Norway
6. Lamps
8. Physical education (initials)
10. Bird
12. I owe you (initials)
13. Cure for poison
15. To rain heavily
17. Type of truck
20. To look through printed matter
22. Ground or earth
24. Fire Department (abbreviation)
25. To give permission
27. New York (postal code)
29. Initials for a steamship

Answer on page 49.

BIRD WATCHERS

Take a walk through these clues and see how many birds you can spot. Each answer will have the name of a bird in it. For example, for the clue "A choosing game," your answer might be "Duck, Duck, Goose." If you get all the answers, you must be a real Bird Brain.

1. A zero: _____

2. Top rank in Boy Scouts: _____

3. Winnie-the-Pooh's human friend: _____

4. Spotty sickness: _____

5. Famous watery ballet: _____

6. Cross in the middle of the street: _____

7. A long metal tool for prying: _____

8. Speak openly and truthfully: _____

9. Sneak away from a room: _____

10. Sweethearts: _____

Answer on page 50.

Illustrated by John Nez

CRUNCH'S LUNCH

Can you help Crunch the Caveman find a safe trail home in time for lunch?

Answer on page 50.

START

FINISH

Illustrated by Lisa Dayer

SYLLABLE SEARCH

A syllable is a single sound that makes up part of a whole word. For instance, the word "apple" has two syllables: the **"ap"** sound and the **"pull"** sound. Together they make apple. "Ladder" is another word with two syllables: the **"lad"** sound and the **"der"** sound. Many things pictured here are words that have two syllables. How many can you find? Remember, look for two sounds in one word, not just two words.

Answer on page 50.

41

SLIPPED SHOTS

How many things can you find wrong
in this picture?

DOT MAGIC

These people are taking the easy way of moving up in the world. To see what they're up to, connect the dots.

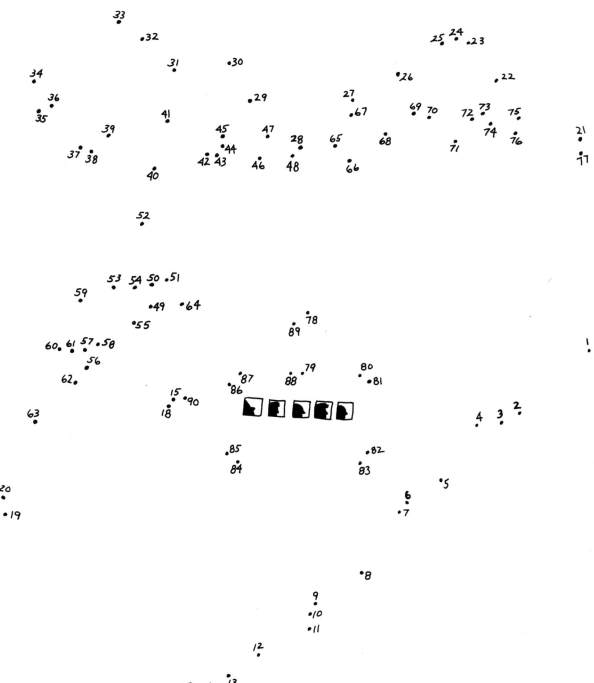

ROUGH RIDER

Albert is riding his bicycle to Zeke's house for the first time. He's having a rough time reading his mom's handwriting, and some of the words even look scrambled. Help Albert pedal from his house, which is marked with an A on the map, to Zeke's house by unscrambling the directions and following the map. Mark Zeke's house with a Z when you find it.

1. Go to the end of **elmtHe dRoa.**
2. Turn right onto **aaeHndblr draveluoB.**
3. Go to the **eodscn** stop sign.
4. Turn right on **flctroeRe oaRd.**
5. Cross two **iesrbdg.**
6. Turn left onto **reTi eeSttr.**
7. Zeke **sevil** in the **tifrs** house on the left.

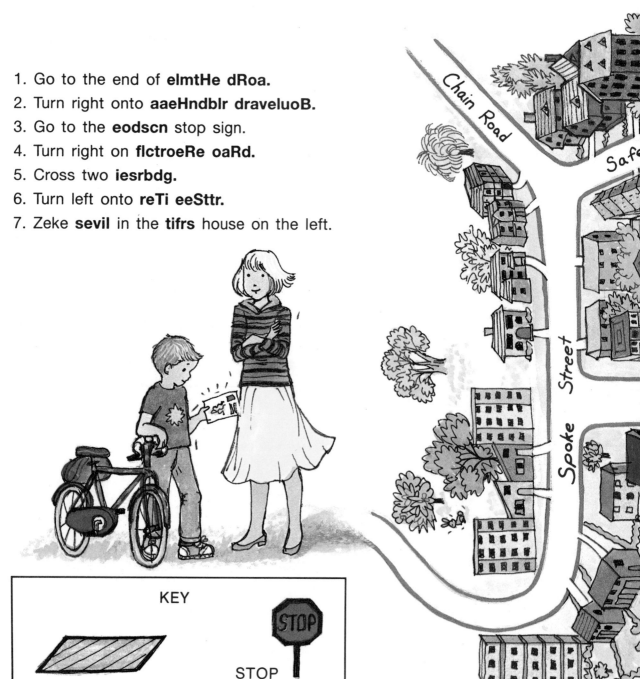

KEY

BRIDGE

STOP SIGN

Illustrated by Belinda Lyon

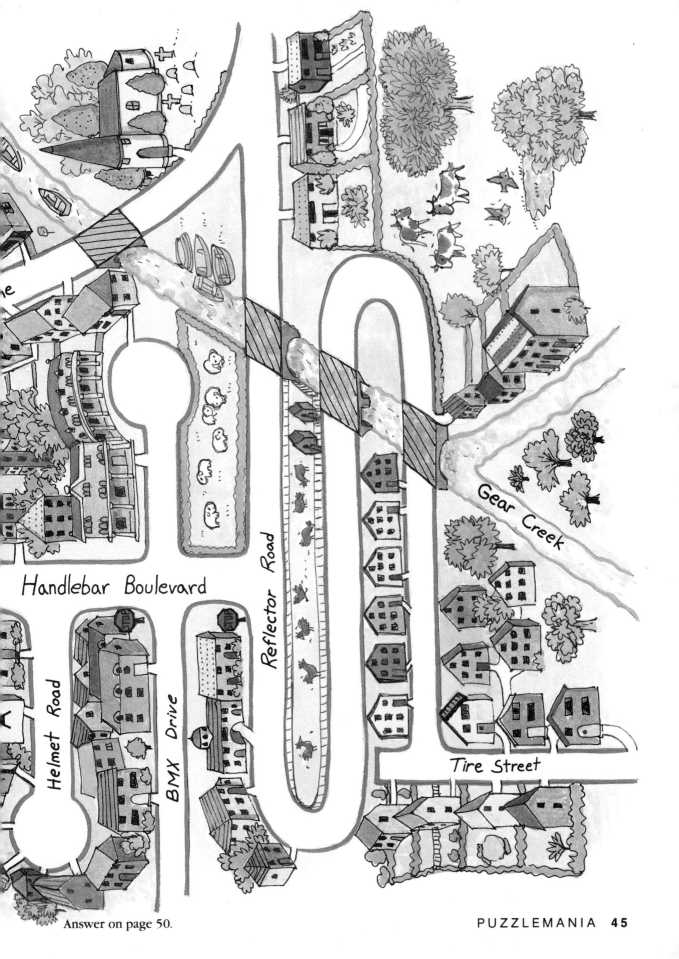

Handlebar Boulevard

Helmet Road

BMX Drive

Reflector Road

Gear Creek

Tire Street

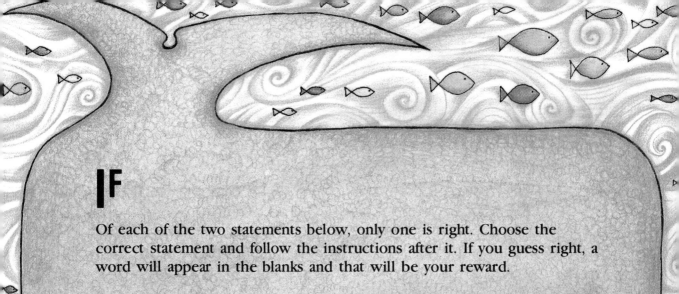

IF

Of each of the two statements below, only one is right. Choose the correct statement and follow the instructions after it. If you guess right, a word will appear in the blanks and that will be your reward.

1. If there are twelve inches in a foot, then #7 is "O."
   If there are ten inches in a foot, then #5 is "C."

2. If a standard deck contains 48 playing cards, then #2 is "Y."
   If a standard deck contains 52 playing cards, then #1 is "L."

3. If a whale is a mammal, then #4 is "L."
   If a whale is not a mammal, then #8 is "B."

4. If Morse Code consists of dots and dashes, then #8 is "P."
   If Semaphore Code consists of dots and dashes, then #4 is "H."

5. If green is a mixture of red and yellow, then #1 is "N."
   If orange is a mixture of red and yellow, then #2 is "O."

6. If you use a microscope to see things in outer space, then #7 is "F."
   If you use a microscope to see things that are very small, then #5 is "I."

7. If it is summer in Australia in December, then #3 is "L."
   If it is winter in Australia in December, then #6 is "M."

8. If there are 31 days in September, then #3 is "A."
   If there are 30 days in September, then #6 is "P."

—— —— —— —— —— —— —— ——
 1   2   3   4   5   6   7   8

Answer on page 50.

ANSWERS

CATERPILLAR COUNTER (page 3)

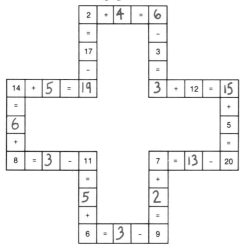

2	+	**4**	=	**6**	

Column down (left): 2 = 17 - ... 14 + **5** = **19**
3 + 12 = **15**

```
  2  +  4  =  6
  =         -
 17         3
  -         =
 14 + 5 = 19    3 + 12 = 15
  =              +
  6              5
  +              =
  8 = 3 - 11    7 = 13 - 20
        =              +
        5              2
        +              =
        6 = 3 - 9
```

PAINT PUZZLE (pages 4-5)

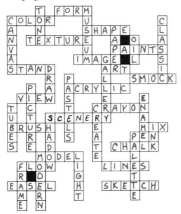

ROW, ROW, ROW (page 6)

menorah   banner   tree
(Hanukkah) (New Year) (Christmas)

dog

snow

fireplace

gifts

piano

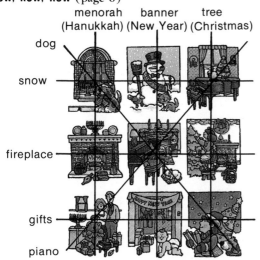

INSTANT PICTURE (page 7)

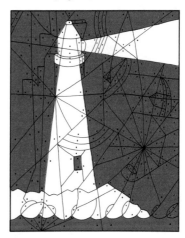

WALKIE-TALKIES (page 10)
1-A   2-D   3-C   4-B

BLUEPRINT BLUNDERS (page 11)
Get one LONG piece of WOOD.
CUT out FIVE sections of equal SIZE, each ONE foot by ONE foot.
Drill a HOLE in the MIDDLE of ONE of these sections. This will be USED as the FRONT.
USE another section as the BASE. Carefully NAIL the other FOUR sections to the sides to form a BOX. Now CUT a section TWELVE inches by EIGHTEEN inches.
NAIL this to the top of the BOX with the extra SIX inches hanging over the FRONT.
Add a DOWEL as a PERCH, and you'll have a brand new BIRDHOUSE.

FARM FUN (pages 12-13)

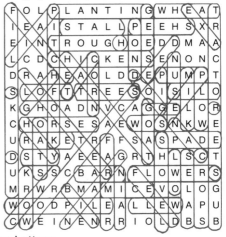

Leftover Letters:
OLD MACDONALD HAD A FARM, E-I-E-I-O

THE WILD WEST (pages 14-15)
A E D H B F C L G J I K

WHAT AM I? (page 16)
Rabbit

DOT'S DEPARTMENT STORE (page 17)

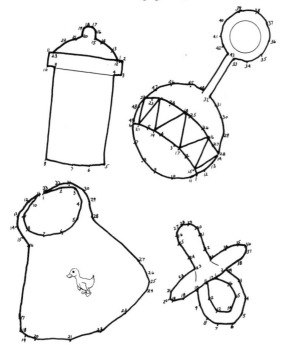

FOOD FOR THOUGHT (pages 18-19)
If I have five potatoes and have to divide them equally between three people, what should I do?

Mash them first.

CATEGORY CAPER (page 20)
1. shapes
2. dogs
3. fish
4. plants
5. clothing
6. toys

SEA CHOOSE (pages 22-23)

TABLE TROUBLE (page 24)
The turkey, roast beef and apple pie are on the ends of the table (Clue 1). The steamed vegetables are also at one end, since they are an even number, but not #4 or #6 (Clue 3). Therefore, the inner four plates must contain soup, gravy, salad, and rice, in some order.

Clue 2 says the soup is directly across from and one number less than the salad. That means it can only be #3 or #5. But the soup must also be to the left of the gravy. Since the gravy can only be an inner plate, it must be #5, and to the left, #3 must be the soup. Directly across is the salad, which must be #4. Only the rice is left to go in #6.

Clue 4 says the rice is next to the turkey. The turkey is on the end (Clue 1), so it must be #8. Roast beef is on the same end, so it goes on #7.

Only #1 and #2 are left. Steamed vegetables go on the even number (Clue 3), which is #2. That leaves #1 for the apple pie.

1. apple pie
2. steamed vegetables
3. soup
4. salad
5. gravy
6. rice
7. roast beef
8. turkey

SQUARE DANCE MEMORIES (page 26)
1. Yes, corn cobs
2. A scarecrow
3. Three
4. Yellow
5. Five
6. Four
7. No, a fiddler was at the microphone.
8. Green
9. A cow was looking in the window.

WHAT IS IT? (page 26)
A river

WHAT'S IN A WORD? (page 27)
Here are some of the words we found.
You may have found others.

all	hen	lone	well
allow	hew	low	whale
alone	hole	new	wheel
awe	hone	noel	when
awl	how	now	won
eel	howl	one	
eon	lane	owe	
ewe	law	owl	
hale	lawn	own	
hallow	lean	wall	
heal	Leo	wan	
heel	loan	wane	

THE CASE OF THE WANDERING WRENS (pages 28-29)

It was nesting time. Wilma Wren selected a spot under the eaves of a small white house. Using twigs from under the big maple TREE, Wilma constructed a cozy NEST. There she laid six small EGGS. Her warm body kept them safe from the hot rays of the SUN, the strong gales of the WIND, and the chilly drops of RAIN.

One day she heard a pecking sound; the delicate SHELLS cracked open, and six BABY birds appeared. All six had their MOUTHS wide open, so Wilma spread her WINGS and flew off to find food. It took some time, but eventually, right next to a four-leaf CLOVER, she spied a long, juicy WORM. Wilma pulled it out of the ground, and flew happily toward the nest and her hungry children.

Down from the sky she flew . . . only to find that everything had disappeared. The nest! The eaves! The house! Everything was gone.

Wilma was frantic. She called her friends, Billy BLUE Jay and ROBIN Redbreast, for help.

"What has happened?" she cried. "Did a FLYING saucer from another planet come down to steal everything away?"

"We'll help you find your children," said her friends, and all three BIRDS flew off through the treetops. On and on they flew, circling the surrounding areas, until far below they saw the little white HOUSE with the bird's nest still under its eaves. WILMA was very happy, but she couldn't imagine what had happened.

"The explanation is really quite simple," said Billy, who was very wise. "It's just that you chose a rather strange place in which to build your nest."

Just where had Wilma built her nest?

U	N	D	E	R		T	H	E		E	A	V	E	S		O	F		A
1	2	3	4	5		6	7	8		9	10	11	12	13		14	15		16

M	O	B	I	L	E		H	O	M	E
17	18	19	20	21	22		23	24	25	26

STOP, LOOK, AND LIST (page 31)

These are the answers we found. You may have found some others.

Things with Holes
Bagel
Chimney
Lace
Piccolo
Swiss Cheese

Pieces of Jewelry
Bracelet
Charm
Locket
Pendant
Stickpin

Green Vegetables
Broccoli
Celery
Lettuce
Peas
Spinach

PICTURE MIXER (pages 32-33)

PUPPETS ON PARADE (page 34)

5 3
6 1
2 4

ONE MORE TIME (page 35)

1. cone
2. done
3. bone
4. gone
5. honey
6. money
7. alone
8. stones
9. sooner
10. throne
11. honest
12. marooned
13. telephone
14. saxophone

FANCY ANTS (pages 36-37)

BIRD WATCHERS (page 38)

1. Goose egg
2. Eagle Scout
3. Christopher Robin
4. Chicken pox
5. Swan Lake
6. Jaywalk
7. Crowbar
8. Talk turkey
9. Duck out
10. Lovebirds

CRUNCH'S LUNCH (page 39)

SYLLABLE SEARCH (pages 40-41)

Here are some of the words we found. You may have found others.

bedroom	hydrant	pirate
bobber	lettuce	pumpkin
bucket	monkey	rabbit
chimney	mountain	raccoon
garden	necklace	rainbow
giant	pancakes	shovel
giraffe	parrot	sneakers
gopher	penguin	treasure

DOT MAGIC (page 43)

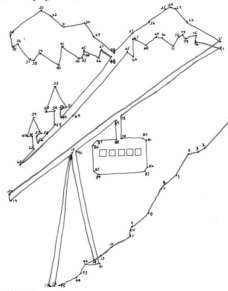

ROUGH RIDER (pages 44-45)

1. Helmet Road
2. Handlebar Boulevard
3. second
4. Reflector Road
5. bridges
6. Tire Street
7. lives, first

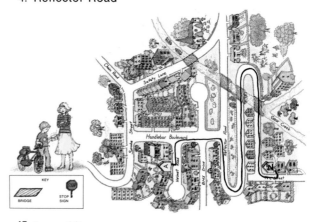

IF (page 46)
Lollipop

Editor: Jeffrey A. O'Hare • **Art Director:** Timothy J. Gillner
Project Director: Pamela Gallo • **Editorial Consultant:** Andrew Gutelle
Design Consultant: Bob Feldgus

Puzzle Contributors
Debbie Driscoll • Roberta Foster • Annette Lingelbach • Isobel Livingstone
Linda Molloy • Jan Onffroy • Anita Sitarski • Jackie Vaughan